# SESMA Picture Dic...

## More than 1000 Illustrations

A simple bilingual picture dictionary with fun illustrations. Great for children ages 5-12.

配有1000余张插图
一本配有插图的简单双语字典。 非常适合5-12岁的儿童。

## Lots of Languages

We are proud to publish the SESMA Picture Dictionary in many different languages from around the world. Find all our language editions online.

多种语言
我们很自豪能够在世界各地以多种不同语言出版SESMA图片词典。在线查找我们所有的语言版本。

**Hello** Привет こんにちは **Ciao** **Bonjour** ولى **Sawubona** 여보세요 **Hola** 你好 **Hallo** Olá

## BilingualDictionaries.com

## Buy Now

The new and improved SESMA Picture Dictionary is back! Purchase bilingual educational materials in over 50 languages.

立即购买
全新改进版SESMA图片字典又回来了！ 购买拥有50余种语言的双语教育资料。

# Table of Contents

# Table of Contents

# Numbers

| 0 | 1 | 2 | 3 |
|---|---|---|---|
| **zero**<br>零 | **one**<br>一 | **two**<br>二 | **three**<br>三 |

| 4 | 5 | 6 | 7 |
|---|---|---|---|
| **four**<br>四 | **five**<br>五 | **six**<br>六 | **seven**<br>七 |

| 8 | 9 | 10 | 11 |
|---|---|---|---|
| **eight**<br>八 | **nine**<br>九 | **ten**<br>十 | **eleven**<br>十一 |

| 12 | 13 | 14 | 15 |
|---|---|---|---|
| **twelve**<br>十二 | **thirteen**<br>十三 | **fourteen**<br>十四 | **fifteen**<br>十五 |

| 16 | 17 | 18 | 19 |
|---|---|---|---|
| **sixteen**<br>十六 | **seventeen**<br>十七 | **eighteen**<br>十八 | **nineteen**<br>十九 |

| 20 | 30 | 40 | 50 |
|---|---|---|---|
| **twenty**<br>二十 | **thirty**<br>三十 | **forty**<br>四十 | **fifty**<br>五十 |

| 60 | 70 | 80 | 90 |
|---|---|---|---|
| **sixty**<br>六十 | **seventy**<br>七十 | **eighty**<br>八十 | **ninety**<br>九十 |

数字

# Numbers

## 100
**one hundred**
一百

## 1,000
**one thousand**
一千

## 1,000,000
**one million**
一百万

## 1,000,000,000
**one billion**
十亿

## 1st
**first**
第一

## 2nd
**second**
第二

## 3rd
**third**
第三

## 4th
**fourth**
第四

## 5th
**fifth**
第五

## 6th
**sixth**
第六

## 7th
**seventh**
第七

## 8th
**eighth**
第八

## 9th
**ninth**
第九

## 10th
**tenth**
第十

## 11th
**eleventh**
第十一

## 12th
**twelfth**
第十二

## 13th
**thirteenth**
第十三

## 14th
**fourteenth**
第十四

## 15th
**fifteenth**
第十五

## 16th
**sixteenth**
第十六

## 17th
**seventeenth**
第十七

## 18th
**eighteenth**
第十八

## 19th
**nineteenth**
第十九

## 20th
**twentieth**
第二十

数字

# Colors

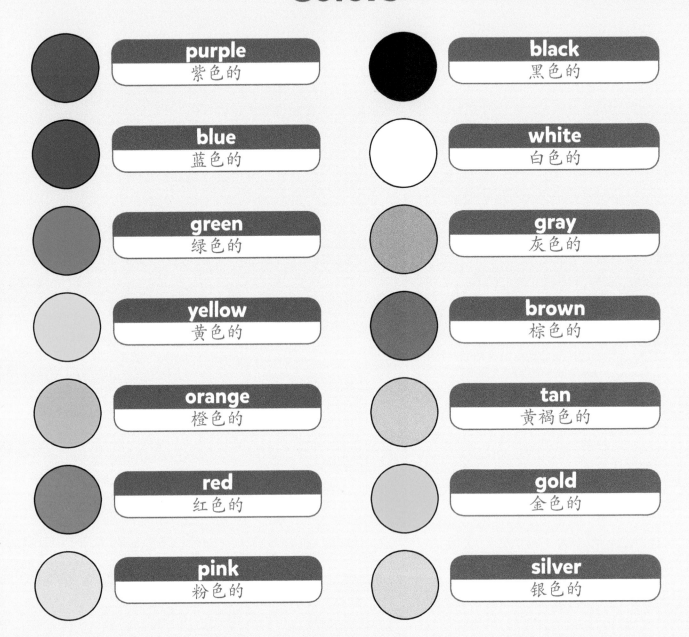

| | purple 紫色的 | | black 黑色的 |
| blue 蓝色的 | | white 白色的 |
| green 绿色的 | | gray 灰色的 |
| yellow 黄色的 | | brown 棕色的 |
| orange 橙色的 | | tan 黄褐色的 |
| red 红色的 | | gold 金色的 |
| pink 粉色的 | | silver 银色的 |

颜色

# Shapes

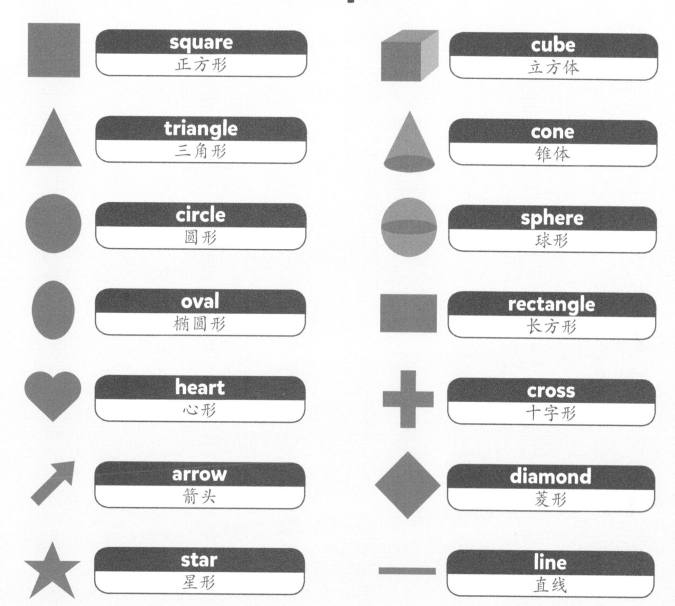

| | | | | |
|---|---|---|---|---|
| square 正方形 | | cube 立方体 | | |
| triangle 三角形 | | cone 锥体 | | |
| circle 圆形 | | sphere 球形 | | |
| oval 椭圆形 | | rectangle 长方形 | | |
| heart 心形 | | cross 十字形 | | |
| arrow 箭头 | | diamond 菱形 | | |
| star 星形 | | line 直线 | | |

形状

# Calendar

### calendar
日历

**12/31/1999**

### date
日期

**12/31/1999**

### month
月

**12/31/1999**

### day
天

**12/31/1999**

### year
年

### January
一月

### February
二月

### March
三月

### April
四月

### May
五月

### June
六月

### July
七月

### August
八月

### September
九月

### October
十月

### November
十一月

### December
十二月

日历

# Calendar

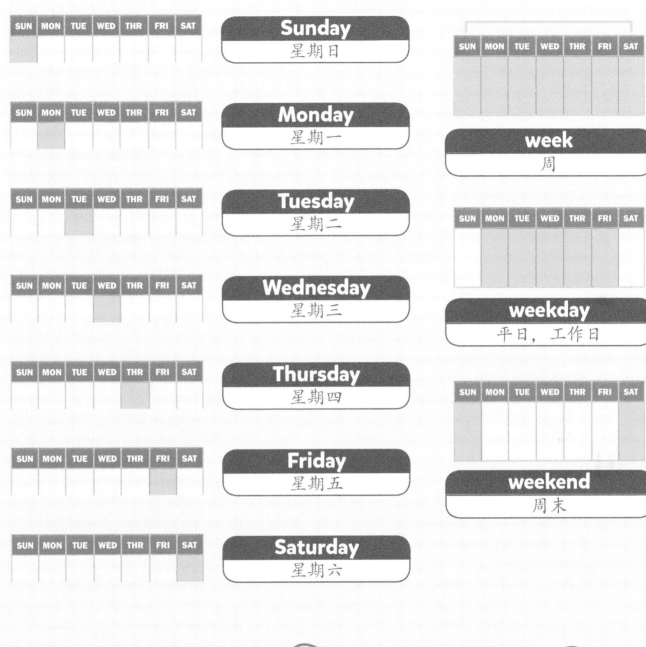

| SUN | MON | TUE | WED | THR | FRI | SAT |
| --- | --- | --- | --- | --- | --- | --- |

**Sunday**
星期日

**Monday**
星期一

**Tuesday**
星期二

**Wednesday**
星期三

**Thursday**
星期四

**Friday**
星期五

**Saturday**
星期六

**week**
周

**weekday**
平日，工作日

**weekend**
周末

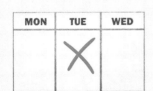

**today**
今天

**yesterday**
昨天

**tomorrow**
明天

日历

# Greetings

**hello**
你好

**goodbye**
再见

**please**
请

**thank you**
谢谢

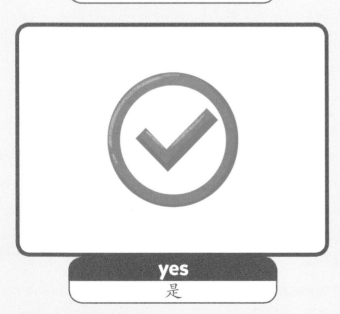

**yes**
是

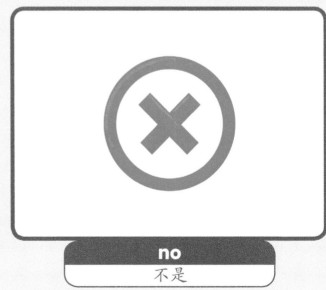

**no**
不是

问候

# Questions ?

**who**
谁

**what**
什么

**when**
什么时候

**where**
在哪里

**why**
为什么

**how**
如何

问题

# When?

**time**
时间

**twelve o' clock**
十二点

**one o' clock**
一点

**two o'clock**
两点

**three o'clock**
三点

**four o'clock**
四点

**five o'clock**
五点

**six o'clock**
六点

**seven o'clock**
七点

**eight o'clock**
八点

**nine o'clock**
九点

**ten o'clock**
十点

**eleven o'clock**
十一点

什么时候?

# When?

**sunrise**
日出

**noon**
中午

**sunset**
日落

**midnight**
午夜

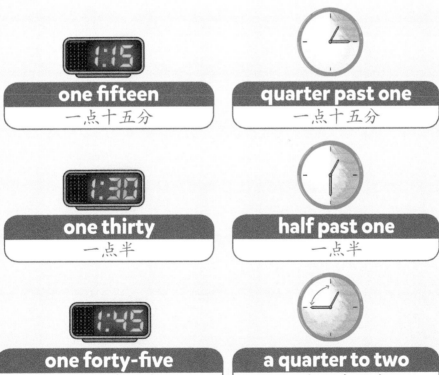

**one fifteen**
一点十五分

**quarter past one**
一点十五分

**one thirty**
一点半

**half past one**
一点半

**one forty-five**
一点四十五分

**a quarter to two**
一点四十五分

**hour**
小时

**minute**
分钟

**second**
秒

什么时候?

# Where?

**up**
向上

**down**
向下

**left**
向左

**right**
向右

**top**
顶部

**bottom**
底部

**front**
前面

**back**
后面

**near**
近的

**far**
远的

在哪里？

# Where?

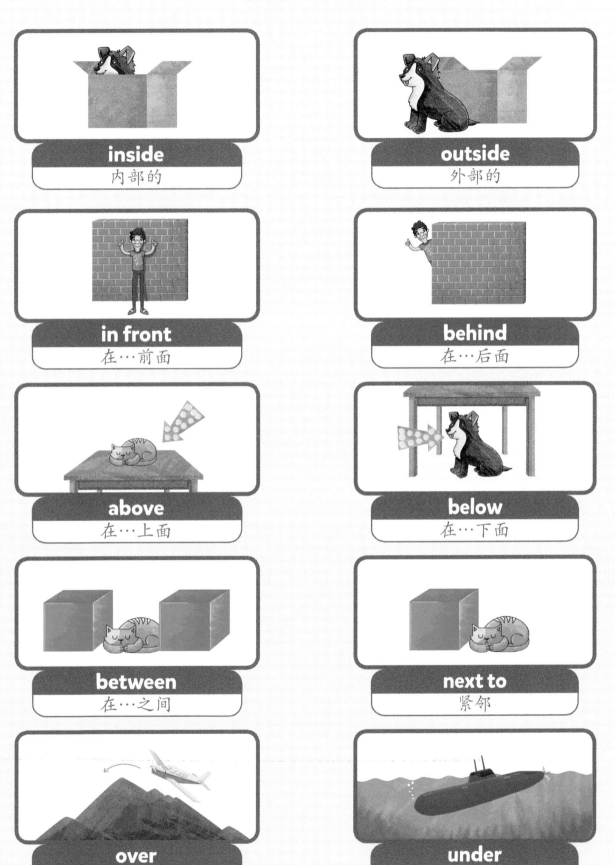

**inside**
内部的

**outside**
外部的

**in front**
在…前面

**behind**
在…后面

**above**
在…上面

**below**
在…下面

**between**
在…之间

**next to**
紧邻

**over**
在…上面

**under**
在…下面

在哪里？

# Money (USA)

$1.00

**dollar**
美元

$0.66

**sixty-six cents**
六十六分

$0.01

**penny**
一分钱

$0.33

**thirty-three cents**
三十三分

$0.05

**nickel**
五分钱

$0.10

**dime**
十分钱

$1.26

**one dollar and twenty-six cents**
一美元二十六美分

$0.25

**quarter**
二十五分

# Chapter 1
# Family

第一章

家人

# Family

### 1. grandmother

### 2. grandfather

### 3. aunt

### 4. mother

### 5. father

### 6. uncle

### 7. brother

### 8. sister

### 9. cousin

| 1. 祖母，外祖母 | 2. 祖父，外祖父 | 3. 阿姨，婶婶，姑妈 |
|---|---|---|
| 4. 妈妈 | 5. 爸爸 | 6. 叔叔，伯伯，舅舅 |
| 7. 哥，弟 | 8. 姐，妹 | 9. 堂（表）兄、弟、姐或妹 |

家人

# Family

## 1. parents

## 2. children

## 3. husband and wife

## 4. son and daughter

## 5. niece and nephew

1. 父母

2. 儿童，孩子

3. 丈夫和妻子

4. 儿子和女儿

5. 侄子和侄女，外甥和外甥女

家人

# Family · Age

### 1. baby

### 2. child

### 3. teenager

### 4. adult

### 5. senior

### 6. woman

### 7. girl

### 8. boy

### 9. man

| 1. 婴儿 | 2. 儿童，孩子 | 3. 青少年 |
| --- | --- | --- |
| 4. 成人 | 5. 老人 | 6. 女人 |
| 7. 女孩 | 8. 男孩 | 9. 男人 |

家人 · 年龄

# Family · Description

**1. handsome**

**2. pretty**

**3. ugly**

**4. skinny**

**5. tall**

**6. young**

**7. fat**

**8. short**

**9. old**

| 1. 英俊的 | 2. 漂亮的 | 3. 丑陋的 |
| --- | --- | --- |
| 4. 消瘦的 | 5. 高的 | 6. 年轻的 |
| 7. 肥的，胖的 | 8. 短的，矮的 | 9. 老的，旧的 |

描述 · 年龄

# Family · Birthday

**1. birthday**

**2. cake**

**3. candle**

**4. balloon**

**5. gift**

**6. party**

**7. friend**

**8. game**

**9. fun**

| 1. 生日 | 2. 蛋糕 | 3. 蜡烛 |
| 4. 气球 | 5. 礼物 | 6. 派对 |
| 7. 朋友 | 8. 游戏 | 9. 有趣的 |

# Family · Wedding

### 1. wedding

### 2. bride

### 3. groom

### 4. to cry

### 5. to dance

### 6. to laugh

### 7. to love

### 8. to kiss

### 9. to hug

| 1. 婚礼 | 2. 新娘 | 3. 新郎 |
| --- | --- | --- |
| 4. 哭 | 5. 跳舞 | 6. 笑 |
| 7. 爱 | 8. 吻 | 9. 拥抱 |

家人 · 婚礼

# Family · Emotions

**1. happy**

**2. sad**

**3. scared**

**4. angry**

**5. surprised**

**6. excited**

**7. embarrassed**

**8. proud**

**9. shy**

| 1. 快乐的 | 2. 伤心的 | 3. 害怕的 |
| --- | --- | --- |
| 4. 生气的 | 5. 惊讶的 | 6. 兴奋的 |
| 7. 尴尬的 | 8. 骄傲的 | 9. 害羞的 |

家人 · 情绪

# Chapter 2
# Home

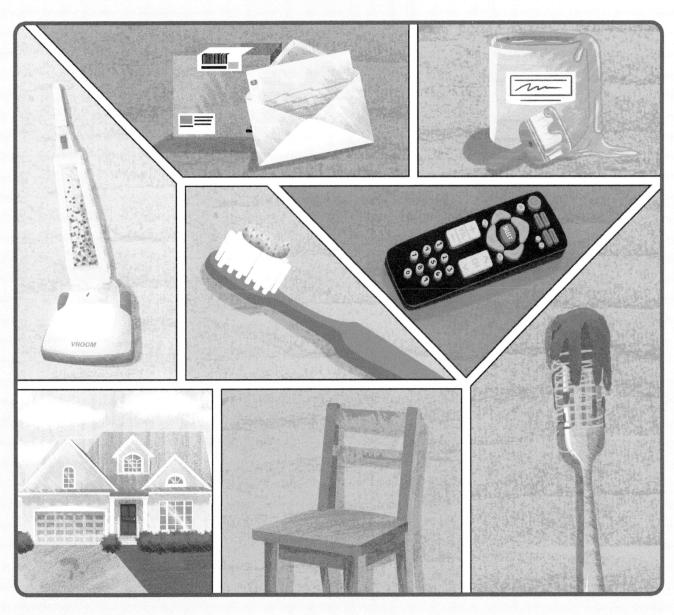

第二章
家

# Home

### 1.house

### 2.apartment

### 3.door

### 4.window

### 5.doorknob

### 6.doorbell

### 7.key

### 8.to knock

### 9.to ring
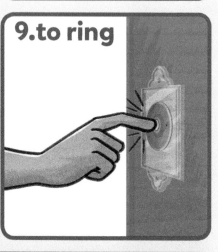

| | | |
|---|---|---|
| 1.房子 | 2.公寓 | 3.门 |
| 4.窗户 | 5.门把手 | 6.门铃 |
| 7.钥匙 | 8.敲 | 9.按门铃 |

家

# Home

**1.stairs**

**2.roof**

**3.chimney**

**4.gate**

**5.garage**

**6.fence**

**7.mailbox**

**8.mail**

**9.to receive**

| 1.楼梯 | 2.屋顶 | 3.烟囱 |
| --- | --- | --- |
| 4.大门 | 5.车库 | 6.篱笆 |
| 7.邮箱 | 8.邮件 | 9.接收 |

家

# Home

**1. kitchen**

**2. bedroom**

**3. bathroom**

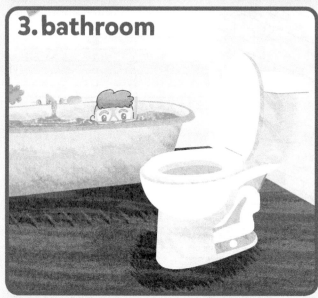

**4. living room**

**5. yard**

1. 厨房

2. 卧式

3. 卫生间

4. 起居室

5. 庭院

家

# Home

## 1. neighbor

## 2. to meet

## 3. to invite

You're invited!

## 4. to wave

1. 邻居

2. 认识，遇见

3. 邀请

4. 挥手

5. 玩

## 5. to play

家

# Home · Kitchen

### 1.refrigerator

### 2.dishwasher

### 3.microwave

### 4.toaster

### 5.stove

### 6.oven

### 7.sink

### 8.counter

### 9.cupboard

| 1.冰箱 | 2.洗碗机 | 3.微波炉 |
| --- | --- | --- |
| 4.烤面包机 | 5.炉子 | 6.烤箱 |
| 7.洗涤槽 | 8.台面 | 9.橱柜 |

家 · 厨房

# Home · Kitchen

**1.plate**

**2.bowl**

**3.cup**

**4.knife**
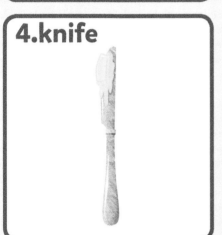

**5.fork**

**6.spoon**

**7.table**

**8.chair**

**9.napkin**

| 1.盘子 | 2.碗 | 3.杯子 |
| --- | --- | --- |
| 4.刀 | 5.叉 | 6.勺子 |
| 7.桌子 | 8.椅子 | 9.餐巾纸 |

家 · 厨房

# Home · Bedroom

**1.bed**

**2.pillow**

**3.blanket**

**4.dresser**

**5.nightstand**

**6.lamp**

**7.closet**

**8.poster**

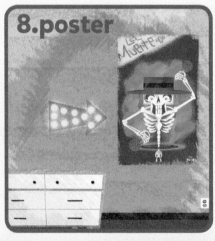

**9.light**

| 1.床 | 2.枕头 | 3.毯子 |
|------|--------|--------|
| 4.梳妆台 | 5.床头柜 | 6.灯 |
| 7.壁柜 | 8.海报 | 9.夜灯 |

家 · 卧室

# Home · Bedroom

### 1. dream

### 2. nightmare

### 3. tired

### 4. awake

1. 梦

2. 噩梦

3. 累的

4. 醒着的

5. 睡觉

### 5. to sleep

家 · 卧室

# Home · Bathroom

**1.shower**

**2.bathtub**

**3.faucet**

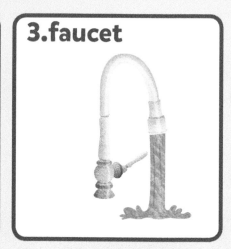

**4.mirror**

**5.toilet**

**6.toilet paper**

**7.hamper**

**8.comb**

**9.soap**

| 1.淋浴 | 2.浴缸 | 3.水龙头 |
| --- | --- | --- |
| 4.镜子 | 5.厕所 | 6.厕纸 |
| 7.洗衣篮 | 8.梳子 | 9.肥皂 |

家 · 卫生间

# Home • Bathroom

## 1.toothbrush

## 2.toothpaste

## 3.towel
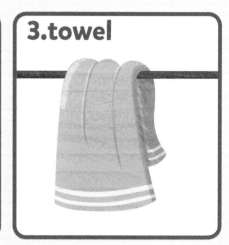

## 4.floss
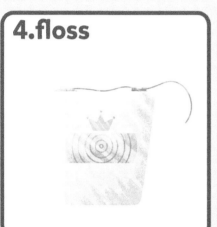

## 5.wet

## 6.dry

## 7.lotion

## 8.clean

## 9.dirty

| 1.牙刷 | 2.牙膏 | 3.毛巾 |
| 4.牙线 | 5.湿的 | 6.干的 |
| 7.沐浴乳 | 8.干净的 | 9.脏的 |

家 · 卫生间

# Home · Bathroom

## 1. to open
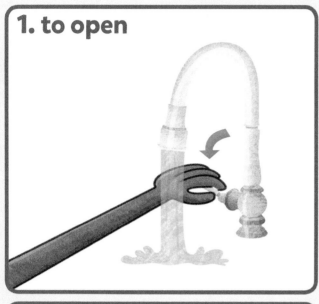

## 2. to close
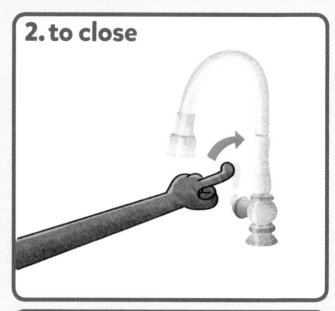

## 3. to comb

## 4. to brush

## 5. to shower

1. 打开

2. 关闭

3. 用梳子梳

4. 刷

5. 淋浴

家 · 卫生间

# Home · Living Room

### 1.wall

### 2.floor

### 3.ceiling

### 4.couch

### 5.carpet

### 6.outlet

### 7.fireplace

### 8.painting

### 9.switch

| 1.墙 | 2.地板 | 3.天花板 |
|---|---|---|
| 4.长沙发 | 5.地毯 | 6.电源插座 |
| 7.壁炉 | 8.油画 | 9.开关 |

家 · 起居室

# Home · Living Room

### 1.television

### 2.tablet

### 3.screen

### 4.remote

### 5.video game

### 6.board game

### 7.toy

### 8.off

### 9.on
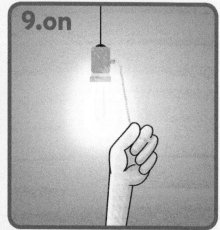

| | | |
|---|---|---|
| 1.电视 | 2.平板电脑 | 3.屏幕 |
| 4.远程 | 5.电子游戏 | 6.棋盘游戏 |
| 7.玩具 | 8.关 | 9.开 |

家 · 卫生间

# Home · Living Room

**1. together**

**2. alone**

**3. to watch**

**4. to cheer**

WOOOOOO!!

1. 一起

2. 单独

3. 观看

4. 欢呼

5. 舒适的

**5. comfortable**

# Home · Yard

### 1.lawn

### 2.garden

### 3.barbecue

### 4.lawn mower

### 5.trash

### 6.hose

### 7.dog house

### 8.tree house

### 9.sprinkler

| 1.草坪 | 2.花园 | 3.烧烤架 |
| --- | --- | --- |
| 4.割草机 | 5.垃圾 | 6.软管 |
| 7.狗屋 | 8.树上小屋 | 9.洒水器 |

家 · 庭院

# Home · Garage

### 1. paint

### 2. ladder

### 3. cooler

### 4. fan

### 5. box

### 6. bag

### 7. to lift

### 8. to carry

### 9. to fall

| 1. 油漆 | 2. 梯子 | 3. 冷却器 |
| --- | --- | --- |
| 4. 风扇 | 5. 盒子 | 6. 袋子 |
| 7. 举起 | 8. 携带 | 9. 倒下 |

家 · 车库

# Home · Tool

### 1.hammer

### 2.nail

### 3.screwdriver

### 4.power drill

### 5.toolbox

### 6.wrench

### 7.tape

### 8.to break

### 9.to fix

| | | |
|---|---|---|
| 1.锤子 | 2.钉子 | 3.螺丝刀 |
| 4.电钻 | 5.工具箱 | 6.扳手 |
| 7.破开 | 8.卷尺 | 9.修理 |

家 · 工具

# Home · Clean

### 1.broom

### 2.dustpan

### 3.mop
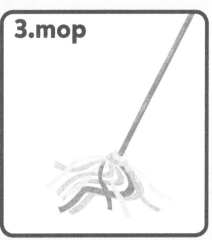

### 4.sponge

### 5.vacuum
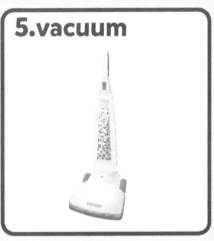

### 6.bucket

### 7.cleaner

### 8.duster

### 9.paper towel

| 1.扫帚 | 2.垃圾铲 | 3.拖把 |
| --- | --- | --- |
| 4.海绵 | 5.吸尘器 | 6.桶 |
| 7.清洁剂 | 8.抹布 | 9.纸巾 |

家 · 清洁

# Home · Clean

**1. to spray**

**2. to wipe**

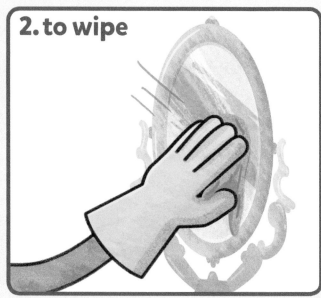

**3. to sweep**

**4. to scrub**

**5. to clean**

1. 喷

2. 喷

3. 扫

4. 擦洗

5. 清空

家 · 清洁

# Chapter 3
# Clothes

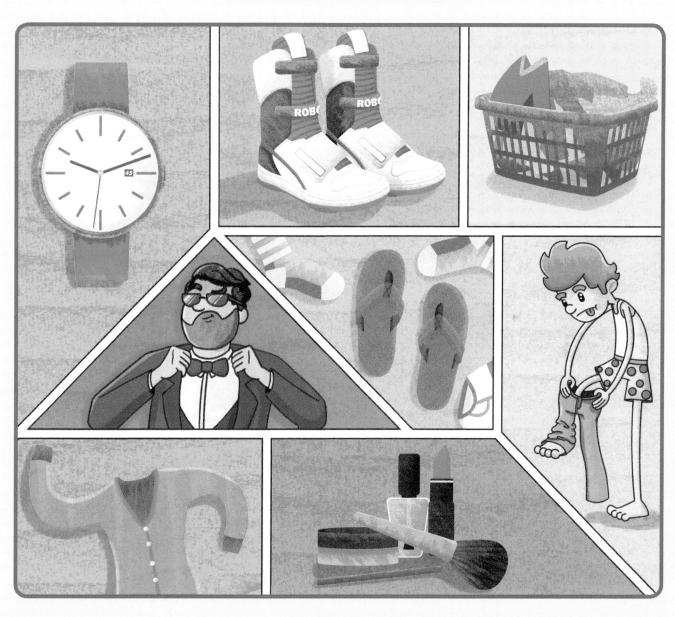

第三章
衣服

# Clothes

### 1. shirt

### 2. pants

### 3. shorts

### 4. underwear

### 5. sock
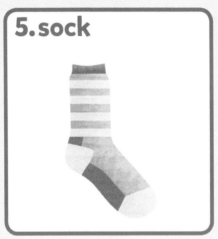

### 6. shoes

### 7. sweater

### 8. jacket

### 9. hat

| 1. 衬衫 | 2. 长裤 | 3. 短裤 |
| --- | --- | --- |
| 4. 内衣 | 5. 短袜 | 6. 鞋 |
| 7. 毛衣 | 8. 夹克衫 | 9. 帽子 |

衣服

# Clothes

**1. sandals**

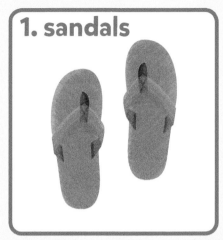

**2. boots**

**3. sneakers**

**4. heel**

**5. sole**

**6. shoelace**

**7. to tie**

**8. to put on**

**9. to take off**

| 1. 凉鞋 | 2. 靴子 | 3. 运动鞋 |
| 4. 脚踝 | 5. 鞋底 | 6. 鞋带 |
| 7. 系上 | 8. 穿上 | 9. 脱下 |

衣服

# Clothes · Girls

**1. dress**

**2. skirt**

**3. bikini**

**4. make-up**

**5. purse**

1. 连衣裙

2. 短裙

3. 比基尼

4. 化妆品

5. 钱包

# Clothes · Boys

### 1. jeans

### 2. t-shirt

### 3. baseball cap

### 4. swimming trunks

1. 牛仔裤

2. T恤衫

3. 棒球帽

4. 泳裤

5. 钱包

### 5. wallet

衣服 · 男孩

# Clothes · Accessories

**1. belt**

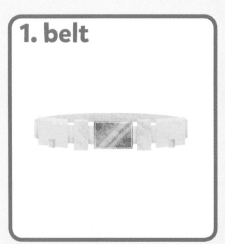

**2. scarf**

**3. watch**

**4. ring**

**5. necklace**

**6. earring**

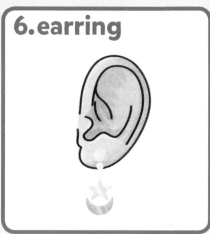

**7. bracelet**

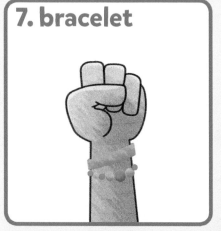

**8. cowboy hat**

**9. glove**

| 1. 皮带 | 2. 围巾 | 3. 手表 |
|---|---|---|
| 4. 戒指 | 5. 项链 | 6. 耳环 |
| 7. 手镯 | 8. 牛仔帽 | 9. 手套 |

衣服 · 配件

# Clothes - Accessories

### 1. pocket

### 2. sleeve

### 3. collar

### 4. hood

### 5. zipper
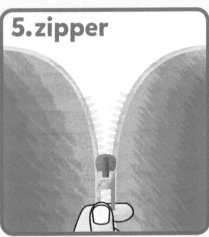

### 6. button

### 7. buckle

### 8. patch

### 9. logo

| 1. 口袋 | 2. 袖子 | 3. 领子 |
| --- | --- | --- |
| 4. 头巾 | 5. 拉链 | 6. 纽扣 |
| 7. 锁扣 | 8. 补丁 | 9. 商标 |

衣服 · 配件

# Clothes · Style

### 1. solid

### 2. striped

### 3. polka dot

### 4. small

### 5. medium

### 6. torn

### 7. large

### 8. extra-large

### 9. stained

1. 纯色的

2. 条纹的

3. 斑点的

4. 小的

5. 中的

6. 破的

7. 大的

8. 特大的

9. 污染的

衣服 · 风格

# Clothes · Style

**1. new**

**2. used**

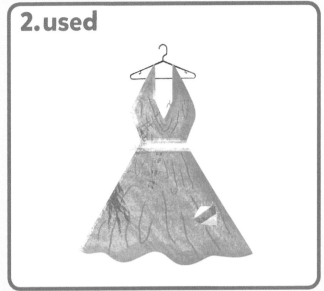

**3. tight**

**4. loose**

1. 新的

2. 用过的

3. 紧的

4. 松的

5. 风格

**5. style**

衣服 · 风格

# Clothes · Laundry

**1. washer**

**2. dryer**

**3. detergent**

**4. basket**

**5. laundry**

**6. hanger**

**7. iron**

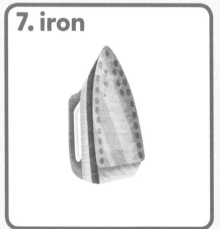

**8. wrinkle**

**9. crease**

| 1. 洗衣机 | 2. 烘干机 | 3. 洗衣液 |
| 4. 篮子 | 5. 要洗的衣服 | 6. 晾衣架 |
| 7. 熨斗 | 8. 褶皱 | 9. 折痕 |

衣服 · 要洗的衣服

# Clothes · Laundry

## 1. to try

## 2. to wear

## 3. to fold

## 4. to put

1. 尝试

2. 穿着

3. 折叠

4. 放置

5. 悬挂

## 5. to hang

衣服 · 要洗的衣服

# Clohes

### 1. uniform

### 2. costume

### 3. pajamas

### 4. suit

### 5. robe

1. 制服

2. 服装

3. 睡衣

4. 西装

5. 礼服

衣服

# Chapter 4
# Food

第四章
食物

# Food

## 1. fruit

## 2. vegetable

## 3. meat

## 4. bread

## 5. condiment

1. 水果

2. 蔬菜

3. 肉

4. 面包

5. 调味品

食物

# Food

### 1. breakfast

### 2. lunch

### 3. dinner

### 4. beverage

1. 早餐

2. 午餐

3. 晚餐

4. 饮料

5. 甜点

### 5. dessert

食物

# Food · Fruit

### 1. apple

### 2. banana

### 3. grapes

### 4. pineapple

### 5. strawberry

### 6. watermelon

### 7. pumpkin

### 8. avocado

### 9. blueberry

| 1. 苹果 | 2. 香蕉 | 3. 葡萄 |
| --- | --- | --- |
| 4. 菠萝 | 5. 草莓 | 6. 西瓜 |
| 7. 南瓜 | 8. 鳄梨 | 9. 蓝莓 |

食物 · 水果

# Food · Fruit

**1. raisin**

**2. orange**

**3. mango**

**4. coconut**

**5. lemon**

**6. lime**

**7. cherry**

**8. juicy**

**9. sour**

| 1. 葡萄干 | 2. 橙子 | 3. 芒果 |
| --- | --- | --- |
| 4. 椰子 | 5. 柠檬 | 6. 青柠 |
| 7. 樱桃 | 8. 多汁的 | 9. 酸的 |

食物 · 水果

# Food · Vegetable

### 1. lettuce

### 2. celery

### 3. carrot

### 4. tomato

### 5. onion

### 6. cucumber

### 7. mushroom

### 8. broccoli

### 9. pickle

| 1. 生菜 | 2. 芹菜 | 3. 胡萝卜 |
| --- | --- | --- |
| 4. 番茄 | 5. 洋葱 | 6. 黄瓜 |
| 7. 蘑菇 | 8. 西兰花 | 9. 泡菜 |

食物 · 蔬菜

# Food · Vegetable

### 1. asparagus

### 2. corn

### 3. potato

### 4. chili pepper

### 5. garlic

### 6. peas

### 7. rotten

### 8. ripe

### 9. fresh

| 1. 芦笋 | 2. 玉米 | 3. 土豆 |
| 4. 红辣椒 | 5. 大蒜 | 6. 豌豆 |
| 7. 烂的 | 8. 成熟的 | 9. 新鲜的 |

食物 · 蔬菜

# Food · Breakfast

**1. egg**

**2. bacon**
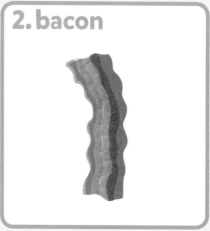

**3. sausage**

**4. ham**

**5. pancakes**

**6. toast**

**7. cereal**

**8. butter**

**9. syrup**

| 1. 蛋 | 2. 燻猪肉 | 3. 香肠 |
| 4. 火腿 | 5. 煎饼 | 6. 烤面包机 |
| 7. 谷物早餐 | 8. 黄油 | 9. 糖浆 |

# Food · Lunch

### 1. hamburger

### 2. fries

### 3. hotdog

### 4. chicken nugget

### 5. pizza
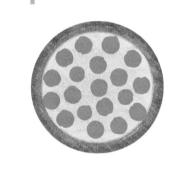

### 6. fish stick

### 7. sandwich

### 8. peanut butter

### 9. jelly

| 1. 汉堡 | 2. 炸薯条 | 3. 热狗 |
| --- | --- | --- |
| 4. 小炸鸡块 | 5. 披萨 | 6. 鱼条 |
| 7. 三明治 | 8. 花生酱 | 9. 果冻 |

食物 · 午餐

# Food · Lunch

## 1. ketchup

## 2. mustard

## 3. mayonnaise

## 4. salt

## 5. cheese

## 6. lunch box

## 7. snack

## 8. spicy

## 9. sweet

| 1. 番茄酱 | 2. 芥末 | 3. 蛋黄酱 |
| --- | --- | --- |
| 4. 盐 | 5. 奶酪 | 6. 饭盒 |
| 7. 小吃 | 8. 辣的 | 9. 甜的 |

# Food · Dinner

### 1. steak

### 2. chicken

### 3. pasta

### 4. soup

### 5. salad

### 6. salad dressing

### 7. beans

### 8. rice

### 9. sushi

| 1. 牛排 | 2. 鸡肉 | 3. 意面 |
| --- | --- | --- |
| 4. 汤 | 5. 沙拉 | 6. 沙拉酱 |
| 7. 豆 | 8. 米饭 | 9. 寿司 |

食物 · 晚餐

# Food · Dessert

**1. candy**

**2. chips**

**3. cookie**

**4. donut**

**5. pie**

**6. cupcake**

**7. frosting**

**8. ice cream**

**9. chocolate**

| 1. 糖果 | 2. 薯片 | 3. 饼干 |
| --- | --- | --- |
| 4. 甜甜圈 | 5. 馅饼 | 6. 纸杯蛋糕 |
| 7. 结霜 | 8. 冰淇淋 | 9. 巧克力 |

食物 · 甜点

# Food · Beverage

**1. juice**

**2. milk**

**3. soda**

**4. tea**

**5. coffee**

**6. water**

**7. ice**

**8. empty**

**9. full**

| 1. 果汁 | 2. 牛奶 | 3. 苏打水 |
| 4. 茶 | 5. 咖啡 | 6. 水 |
| 7. 冰 | 8. 空的 | 9. 满的 |

食物 · 饮料

# Food · Cook

### 1. pan

### 2. pot

### 3. colander

### 4. spatula

### 5. tongs

### 6. ladle
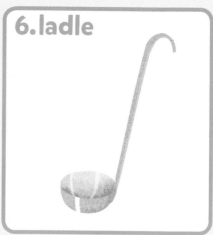

### 7. to prepare

### 8. to cook

### 9. to wash

| 1. 平底锅 | 2. 锅 | 3. 滤器 |
| --- | --- | --- |
| 4. 抹刀 | 5. 钳子 | 6. 长柄勺 |
| 7. 准备 | 8. 烹饪 | 9. 洗 |

食物 · 烹饪

# Food · Cook

### 1. to grill

### 2. to peel

### 3. to stir

### 4. to boil

### 5. to fry

### 6. to bake

### 7. to mix

### 8. to sprinkle

### 9. to heat

| 1. 烤 | 2. 去皮 | 3. 搅拌 |
| 4. 煮 | 5. 煎 | 6. 烘焙 |
| 7. 搅拌 | 8. 撒上 | 9. 加热 |

食物 · 烹饪

# Food · Eat

### 1. to eat

### 2. to drink

### 3. to chew

### 4. to burp

### 5. to pour

### 6. to dip

### 7. hungry

### 8. thirsty

### 9. delicious

| | | |
|---|---|---|
| 1. 吃 | 2. 喝 | 3. 咀嚼 |
| 4. 打嗝 | 5. 倒 | 6. 浸泡 |
| 7. 饿的 | 8. 渴的 | 9. 美味的 |

食物 · 吃

# Chapter 5
# Health

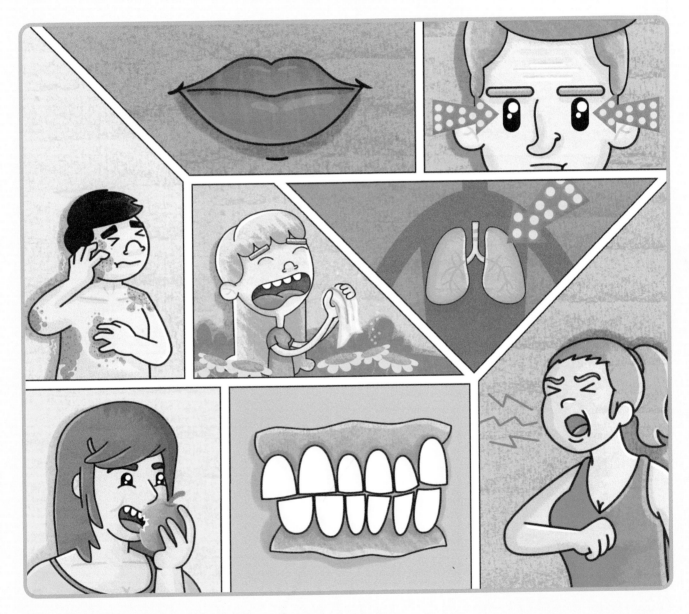

第五章
健康

# Health

### 1. head

### 2. body
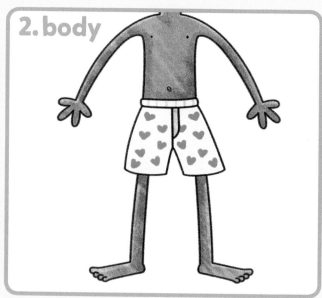

### 3. sick

### 4. hurt

### 5. healthy

1. 头

2. 身体

3. 生病的

4. 受伤的

5. 健康的

健康

# Health

### 1. brain
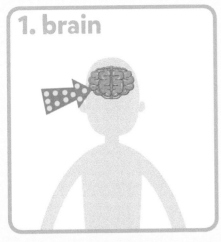

### 2. lungs
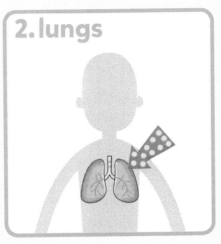

### 3. heart
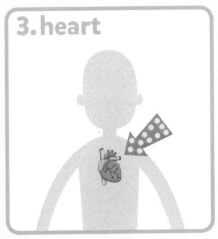

### 4. blood
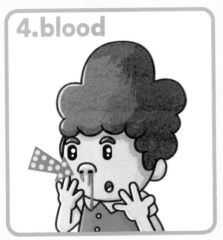

### 5. skin

### 6. muscle

### 7. bone
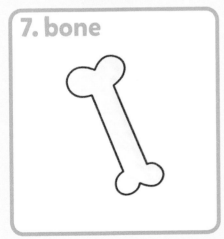

### 8. skull

### 9. skeleton

| 1. 大脑 | 2. 肺 | 3. 心脏 |
| --- | --- | --- |
| 4. 血液 | 5. 皮肤 | 6. 肌肉 |
| 7. 骨头 | 8. 头骨 | 9. 骨架 |

健康

# Health · Head

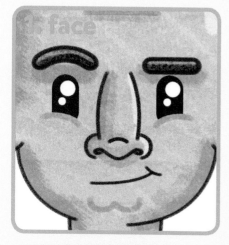
**1. face**

**2. eye**

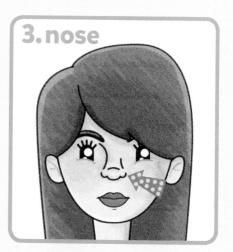
**3. nose**

**4. forehead**

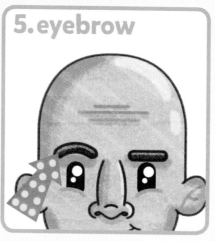
**5. eyebrow**

**6. ear**

**7. cheek**

**8. chin**

**9. hair**

| 1. 脸 | 2. 眼 | 3. 鼻子 |
|---|---|---|
| 4. 前额 | 5. 眉 | 6. 耳 |
| 7. 脸颊 | 8. 下巴 | 9. 头发 |

健康 · 头

# Health · Head

### 1. mouth

### 2. lips

### 3. teeth
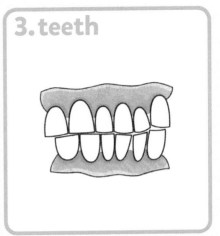

### 4. tongue

### 5. neck

### 6. to talk

### 7. to smile

### 8. to bite

### 9. to lick

| 1. 嘴 | 2. 嘴唇 | 3. 牙齿 |
| --- | --- | --- |
| 4. 舌头 | 5. 脖子 | 6. 说话 |
| 7. 微笑 | 8. 咬 | 9. 舔 |

健康 · 头

# Health · Body

### 1. chest
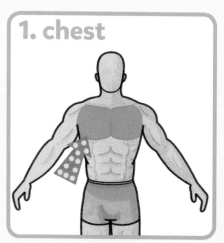

### 2. stomach
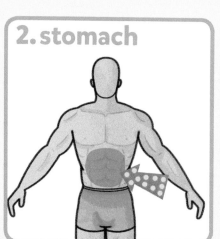

### 3. arm
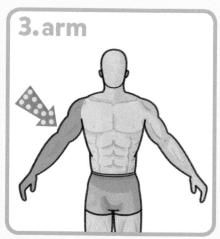

### 4. elbow
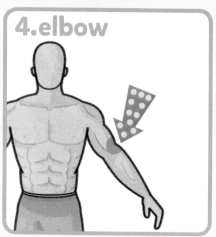

### 5. wrist
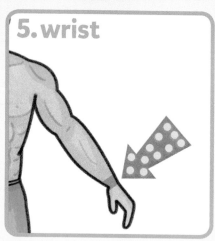

### 6. hand
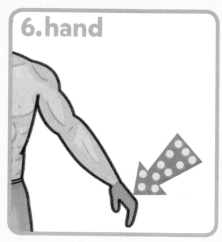

### 7. finger
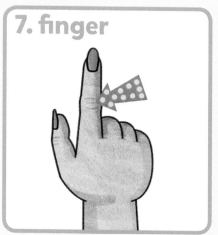

### 8. thumb

### 9. nail

| | | |
|---|---|---|
| 1. 胸部 | 2. 胃 | 3. 臂 |
| 4. 肘 | 5. 腕 | 6. 手 |
| 7. 手指 | 8. 拇指 | 9. 指甲 |

健康 · 身体

# Health · Body

### 1. back
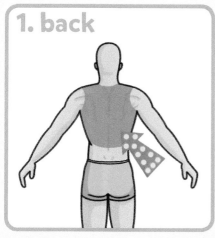

### 2. shoulder
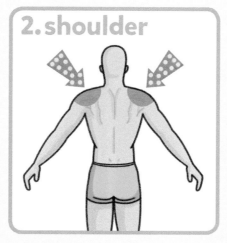

### 3. waist
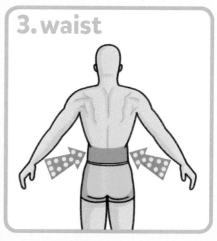

### 4. hips
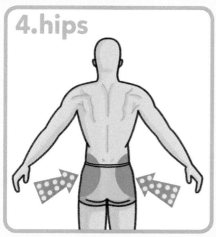

### 5. leg
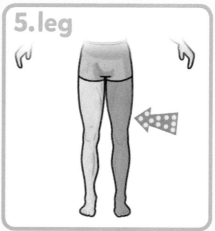

### 6. knee
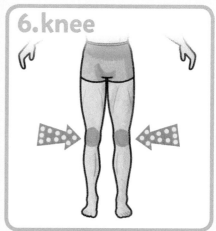

### 7. ankle
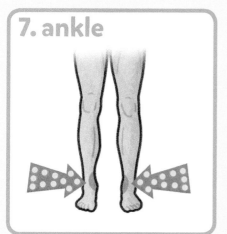

### 8. foot
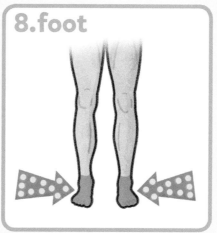

### 9. toe
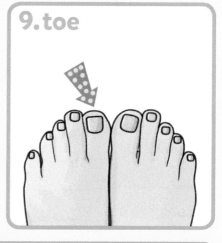

| 1. 背部 | 2. 肩 | 3. 腰 |
|---|---|---|
| 4. 臀部 | 5. 腿 | 6. 膝盖 |
| 7. 脚踝 | 8. 脚 | 9. 脚趾 |

健康 · 身体

# Health · Sick

### 1. cold

### 2. fever
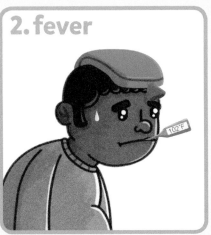

### 3. flu

### 4. headache

### 5. allergy

### 6. stomach ache

### 7. to cough

### 8. to sneeze

### 9. to vomit

| | | |
|---|---|---|
| 1. 感冒 | 2. 发烧 | 3. 流感 |
| 4. 头痛 | 5. 过敏 | 6. 腹痛 |
| 7. 咳嗽 | 8. 打喷嚏 | 9. 呕吐 |

健康 · 生病的

# Health · Hurt

### 1. cut

### 2. bruise

### 3. burn
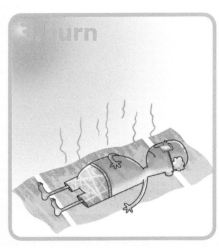

### 4. rash
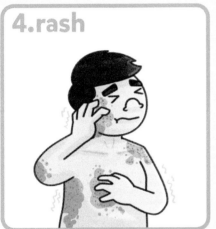

### 5. bite

### 6. pain

### 7. swollen (*finger*)

### 8. broken (*bone*)
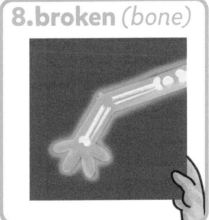

### 9. to bleed
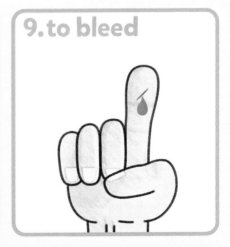

| 1. 割伤 | 2. 挫伤 | 3. 烧伤 |
|---|---|---|
| 4. 皮疹 | 5. 刺痛 | 6. 疼痛 |
| 7. 肿的 | 8. 破裂的 | 9. 流血 |

健康 · 受伤的

# Health · Healthy

## 1. to see

## 2. to hear

## 3. to taste

## 4. to smell

## 5. to touch

## 6. to breathe

## 7. to sweat

## 8. strong

## 9. weak

| | | |
|---|---|---|
| 1. 看到 | 2. 听到 | 3. 尝 |
| 4. 闻 | 5. 触摸 | 6. 呼吸 |
| 7. 出汗 | 8. 强壮的 | 9. 弱的 |

健康 · 健康的

# Chapter 6
# School

第六章
学校

# School

**1. office**

**2. classroom**

**3. cafeteria**

**4. field**

**5. auditorium**

**6. gym**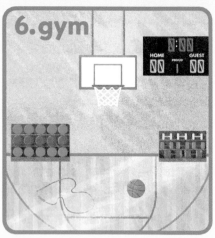

**7. playground**

**8. restroom**

**9. hallway**

| 1. 办公室 | 2. 教室 | 3. 自助餐馆 |
| --- | --- | --- |
| 4. 田野 | 5. 礼堂 | 6. 体育馆 |
| 7. 操场 | 8. 卫生间 | 9. 走廊 |

学校

# School

### 1. principal

### 2. teacher

### 3. student

### 4. janitor

### 5. nurse

### 6. classmate

### 7. guard

### 8. fountain

### 9. locker

| 1. 校长 | 2. 老师 | 3. 学生 |
| --- | --- | --- |
| 4. 清洁工 | 5. 护士 | 6. 同学 |
| 7. 守卫 | 8. 喷泉 | 9. 更衣室 |

学校

# School · Classroom

## 1. whiteboard

## 2. marker

## 3. desk

## 4. projector

## 5. screen

## 6. chair

## 7. clock

## 8. waste basket

## 9. flag

| 1. 白板 | 2. 标记 | 3. 课桌 |
| --- | --- | --- |
| 4. 投影仪 | 5. 屏幕 | 6. 椅子 |
| 7. 时钟 | 8. 垃圾桶 | 9. 旗 |

# School · Classroom

**1. to teach**

**2. to learn**

**3. to study**

**4. to think**

1. 教

2. 学习

3. 读

4. 思考

5. 毕业

**5. to graduate**

学校 · 课堂

# School · Math

### 1. math

### 2. odd

### 3. even

### 4. calculator

07734

### 5. to add
2+2=4

### 6. to subtract
3-1=2

### 7. to multiply

5×2=10

### 8. to divide
8÷4=2

### 9. to equal

| 1. 数学 | 2. 奇的 | 3. 偶的 |
| --- | --- | --- |
| 4. 计算器 | 5. 加 | 6. 减 |
| 7. 乘 | 8. 除 | 9. 等于 |

学校 · 数学

# School · Science

**1. science**

**2. experiment**

**3. scientist**

**4. microscope**

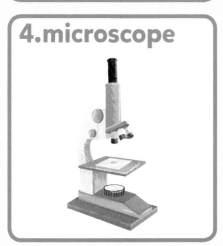

**5. atom**

**6. cell**

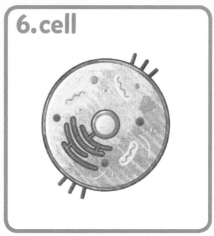

**7. robot**

**8. electricity**

**9. magnet**

| 1. 科学 | 2. 实验 | 3. 科学家 |
| 4. 显微镜 | 5. 原子 | 6. 细胞 |
| 7. 机器人 | 8. 电力 | 9. 磁铁 |

学校 · 科学

# School · English

**1. language**

**2. alphabet**

**3. letter**

**4. word**

**5. sentence**

**6. dictionary**

**7. to listen**

**8. to read**

**9. to write**

| 1. 语言 | 2. 字母表 | 3. 字母 |
| --- | --- | --- |
| 4. 词语 | 5. 句子 | 6. 字典 |
| 7. 听 | 8. 阅读 | 9. 来写 |

学校 · 英语

# School · Lesson

### 1. lesson

### 2. homework

### 3. test

### 4. question
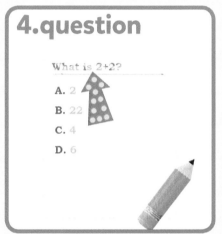

### 5. easy

### 6. difficult

### 7. answer
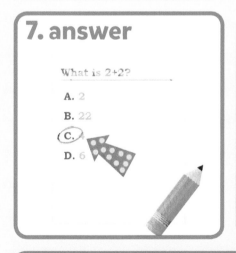

### 8. to remember

### 9. to forget

| 1. 课 | 2. 家庭作业 | 3. 测验 |
| --- | --- | --- |
| 4. 问题 | 5. 简单的 | 6. 难的 |
| 7. 答案 | 8. 记住 | 9. 忘记 |

# School · Supplies

**1. pencil**

**2. pen**

**3. crayon**

**4. backpack**

**5. paper**

**6. eraser**

**7. scissors**

**8. glue**

**9. ruler**

| 1. 铅笔 | 2. 钢笔 | 3. 蜡笔 |
| 4. 背包 | 5. 纸 | 6. 橡皮 |
| 7. 剪刀 | 8. 胶 | 9. 尺 |

学校 · 用品

# School · Supplies

**1. to color**

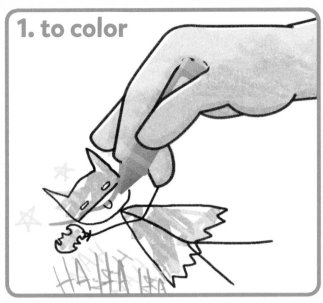

**2. to glue**

**3. to erase**

**4. to cut**

1. 上色

2. 涂胶水

3. 擦除

4. 切割

5. 测量

**5. to measure**

学校 · 用品

# School · Computer

### 1. computer

### 2. laptop

### 3. mouse
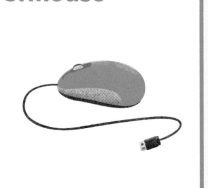

### 4. monitor

### 5. keyboard

### 6. printer

### 7. speaker

### 8. to type

### 9. to select

| 1. 电脑 | 2. 笔记本电脑 | 3. 鼠标 |
| --- | --- | --- |
| 4. 显示器 | 5. 键盘 | 6. 打印机 |
| 7. 扬声器 | 8. 输入 | 9. 选择 |

学校 · 电脑

# School · Internet

**1. internet**

**2. website**

**3. to search**

**4. username**

**5. password**

**6. to log in**

**7. email**

**8. to send**

**9. to download**

| 1. 互联网 | 2. 网站 | 3. 搜索 |
| --- | --- | --- |
| 4. 用户名 | 5. 密码 | 6. 登录 |
| 7. 电子邮件 | 8. 发送 | 9. 下载 |

学校 · 互联网

# School

## 1. elementary

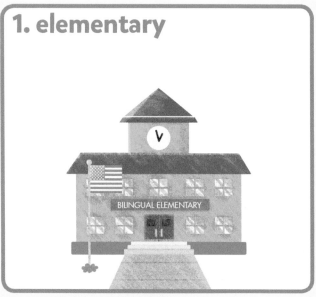

## 2. middle school

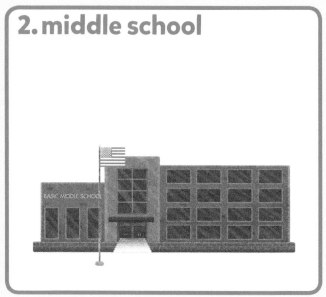

## 3. high school

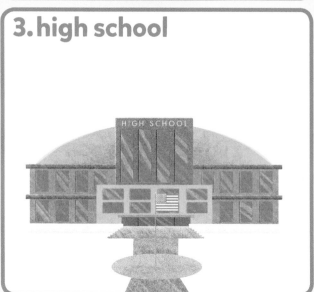

## 4. college

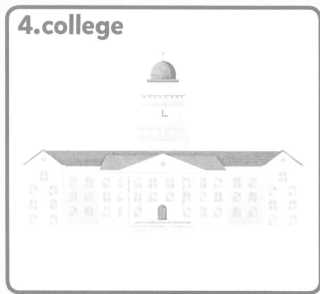

## 5. school bus

1. 小学

2. 中学

3. 高中

4. 大学

5. 校车

# Chapter 7
# City

第七章
城市

# City

**1. city**

**2. church**

**3. post office**

**4. police station**

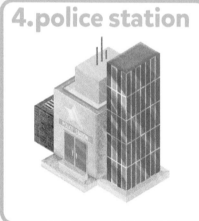

**5. fire station**

**6. city hall**

**7. airport**

**8. hospital**

**9. library**

| 1. 城市 | 2. 教堂 | 3. 邮局 |
| --- | --- | --- |
| 4. 警察局 | 5. 消防局 | 6. 市政厅 |
| 7. 飞机场 | 8. 醫院 | 9. 图书馆 |

城市

# City

**1. bank**

**2. museum**

**3. court house**

**4. auto shop**

**5. gas station**

**6. bus stop**

**7. parking lot**

**8. bridge**

**9. tunnel**

| | | |
|---|---|---|
| 1. 加油站 | 2. 博物馆 | 3. 法院 |
| 4. 汽车店 | 5. 加油站 | 6. 公交车站 |
| 7. 停车场 | 8. 桥 | 9. 隧道 |

城市

# City · Car

**1. car**

**2. truck**

**3. motorcycle**

**4. semi-truck**

**5. garbage truck**

**6. taxi**

**7. bus**

**8. train**

**9. subway**

| 1. 汽车 | 2. 卡车 | 3. 摩托车 |
| --- | --- | --- |
| 4. 半挂车 | 5. 垃圾车 | 6. 出租车 |
| 7. 公交车 | 8. 火车 | 9. 地铁 |

# City · Car

### 1. headlight

### 2. windshield

### 3. bumper

### 4. hood

### 5. license plate

### 6. tire

### 7. engine

### 8. steering wheel

### 9. gas

| | | |
|---|---|---|
| 1. 大灯 | 2. 挡风玻璃 | 3. 保险杠 |
| 4. 车前盖 | 5. 车牌 | 6. 轮胎 |
| 7. 发动机 | 8. 方向盘 | 9. 汽油 |

城市 · 汽车

# City · Traffic

### 1. traffic

### 2. traffic light

### 3. sign

SPEED LIMIT 70

### 4. intersection
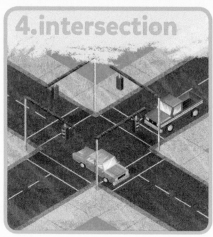

### 5. corner

### 6. sidewalk

### 7. crosswalk

### 8. street

### 9. highway

| 1. 交通 | 2. 交通灯 | 3. 标志 |
|---------|-----------|---------|
| 4. 路口 | 5. 角 | 6. 人行道 |
| 7. 人行横道 | 8. 街 | 9. 高速公路 |

# City · Traffic

### 1. to go

### 2. to stop

### 3. to cross

### 4. to get on

### 5. to get off

### 6. to wait

### 7. to drive

### 8. to park

### 9. to crash

| 1. 去 | 2. 停止 | 3. 横跨 |
|---|---|---|
| 4. 上车 | 5. 下车 | 6. 等待 |
| 7. 驾车 | 8. 停车 | 9. 撞车 |

城市 · 交通

# City · Library

**1. librarian**

**2. book**

**3. magazine**

**4. newspaper**

**5. map**

**6. title**

**7. to look**

**8. to get**

**9. to return**

| 1. 图书管理员 | 2. 书 | 3. 杂志 |
| --- | --- | --- |
| 4. 报纸 | 5. 地图 | 6. 书名 |
| 7. 查看 | 8. 获取 | 9. 返回 |

# City · Hospital

**1. doctor**

**2. patient**

**3. ambulance**

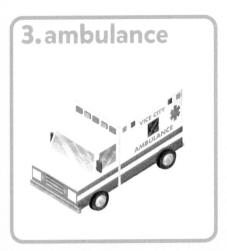

**4. medicine**

**5. crutch**

**6. wheelchair**

**7. injection**

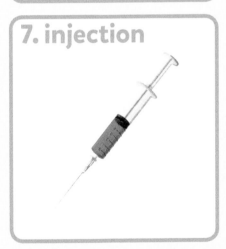

**8. cast**

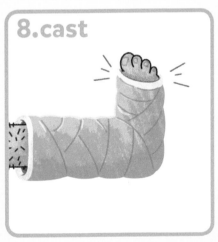

**9. X-ray**

| 1. 医生 | 2. 患者 | 3. 救护车 |
| --- | --- | --- |
| 4. 药 | 5. 拐杖 | 6. 轮椅 |
| 7. 注射 | 8. 石膏 | 9. X-射线 |

# City · Bank

### 1. teller

### 2. money

### 3. coin

### 4. check

### 5. debit card

### 6. PIN number

### 7. to deposit

### 8. to withdraw

### 9. to save

| | | |
|---|---|---|
| 1. 出纳员 | 2. 钱 | 3. 硬币 |
| 4. 支票 | 5. 借记卡 | 6. PIN 编号 |
| 7. 存款 | 8. 取款 | 9. 储蓄 |

# City · Safety

### 1. police car

### 2. crime

### 3. police officer

### 4. fire truck

### 5. fire

### 6. fire fighter

### 7. airplane

### 8. passenger

### 9. pilot

| 1. 警车 | 2. 犯罪 | 3. 警官 |
| --- | --- | --- |
| 4. 消防车 | 5. 火 | 6. 消防员 |
| 7. 飞机 | 8. 乘客 | 9. 飞行员 |

城市 · 安全

# City · Jobs

**1. trash collector**

**2. judge**

**3. mayor**

**4. mail carrier**

**5. driver**

**6. engineer**

**7. security**

**8. architect**

**9. lawyer**

| | | |
|---|---|---|
| 1. 垃圾收集工 | 2. 法官 | 3. 市长 |
| 4. 邮递员 | 5. 司机 | 6. 工程师 |
| 7. 保安 | 8. 建筑师 | 9. 律师 |

城市 · 工作

# Chapter 8
# Life

第八章

生活

# Life · Good

### 1. good

### 2. quiet

### 3. smart

### 4. confident

### 5. to work

1. 好的

2. 安静的

3. 聪明的

4. 有信心的

5. 去工作

生活 · 好的

# Life · Bad

1. bad

2. noisy

3. lazy

4. nervous

1. 坏的

2. 嘈杂的

3. 懒的

4. 紧张的

5. 偷窃

5. to steal

生活 · 坏的

# Life · Store

## 1. mall

## 2. store

## 3. groceries

## 4. cart

## 5. line

## 6. register

## 7. expensive
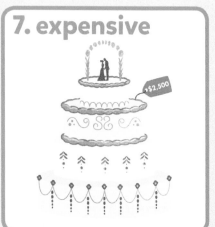

## 8. cheap

## 9. to buy

1. 购物中心

2. 商店

3. 杂货

4. 购物车

5. 队列

6. 登记

7. 昂贵的

8. 低廉的

9. 购买

生活 · 商店

# Life • Restaurant

### 1. chef

### 2. waiter

### 3. customer

### 4. straw
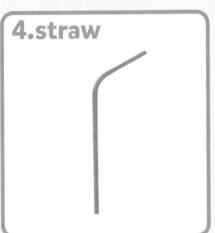

### 5. lid

### 6. menu

### 7. drive-through

### 8. to order

### 9. to ask

| 1. 厨师 | 2. 服务员 | 3. 顾客 |
|---|---|---|
| 4. 稻草 | 5. 盖 | 6. 菜单 |
| 7. 免下车餐厅 | 8. 预订 | 9. 问 |

生活 • 餐厅

# Life · Phone

## 1. cell phone

## 2. to call

## 3. message

## 4. camera

## 5. picture

## 6. battery

## 7. to record

## 8. video

Cat sings the national anthem!!!! WOW!
1,230,930 views

## 9. to charge

| | | |
|---|---|---|
| 1. 手机 | 2. 打电话 | 3. 短信 |
| 4. 相机 | 5. 图片 | 6. 电池 |
| 7. 录音/录像 | 8. 视频 | 9. 充电 |

生活 · 手机

# Life · Music

**1. guitar**

**2. drums**

**3. piano**

**4. violin**

**5. flute**

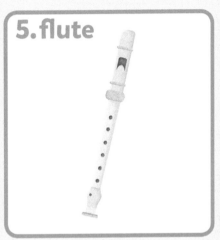

**6. trumpet**

**7. band**

**8. concert**

**9. to sing**

| 1. 吉他 | 2. 鼓 | 3. 钢琴 |
| 4. 小提琴 | 5. 长笛 | 6. 喇叭 |
| 7. 乐队 | 8. 音乐会 | 9. 唱 |

生活 · 音乐

# Life · Entertainment

### 1. movie

### 2. show

### 3. cartoon

### 4. park

### 5. bowling

### 6. arcade

### 7. zoo

### 8. roller coaster
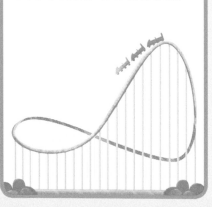

### 9. to ride

| | | |
|---|---|---|
| 1. 电影 | 2. 表演 | 3. 动画片 |
| 4. 公园 | 5. 保龄球 | 6. 游乐场 |
| 7. 动物园 | 8. 过山车 | 9. 骑 |

生活 · 娱乐

# Life · Park

### 1. swing
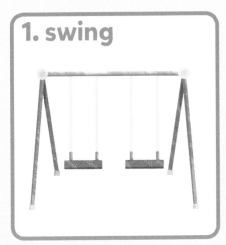

### 2. slide

### 3. monkey bars
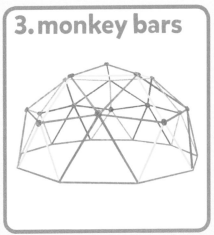

### 4. bench

### 5. to run

### 6. to climb

### 7. to push

### 8. to pull

### 9. to like

| 1. 秋千 | 2. 滑梯 | 3. 攀登架 |
| 4. 长凳 | 5. 跑步 | 6. 攀爬 |
| 7. 推 | 8. 拉 | 9. 喜欢 |

生活 · 公园

# Life · Sports

### 1. baseball

### 2. volleyball

### 3. basketball

### 4. football

### 5. soccer

### 6. hockey

### 7. tennis

### 8. golf

### 9. cricket

| 1. 棒球 | 2. 排球 | 3. 篮球 |
| --- | --- | --- |
| 4. 橄榄球 | 5. 足球 | 6. 曲棍球 |
| 7. 网球 | 8. 高尔夫球 | 9. 板球 |

生活 · 体育

# Life · Sports

### 1. surfing

### 2. snowboarding

### 3. skating

### 4. boxing

### 5. wrestling

### 6. gymnastics

### 7. ring

### 8. stadium

### 9. track

| 1. 冲浪 | 2. 单板滑雪 | 3. 溜冰 |
| --- | --- | --- |
| 4. 拳击 | 5. 摔角 | 6. 体操 |
| 7. 跑道 | 8. 体育场 | 9. 跑道 |

生活 · 体育

# Life · Sports

## 1. uniform

## 2. helmet

## 3. cleats

## 4. bat

## 5. goal

## 6. net

## 7. to stretch

## 8. to exercise

## 9. to practice

| 1. 制服 | 2. 头盔 | 3. 夹板 |
| 4. 球拍 | 5. 球门 | 6. 球网 |
| 7. 伸展 | 8. 锻炼 | 9. 练习 |

生活 · 体育

# Life · Sports

## 1. to win

## 2. to lose

## 3. to score

## 4. to throw

## 5. to catch

## 6. to kick

## 7. to jump

## 8. to race

## 9. to hit

| 1. 赢 | 2. 输 | 3. 得分 |
| 4. 扔 | 5. 抓 | 6. 踢 |
| 7. 跳 | 8. 赛跑 | 9. 打 |

生活 · 体育

# Life · Sports

**1. athlete**

**2. team**

**3. coach**

**4. referee**

**5. fan**

1. 运动员

2. 球队

3. 教练

4. 裁判

5. 球迷

# Chapter 9
# Nature

第九章
大自然

# Nature · Plants

### 1. tree

### 2. bush

### 3. plant

### 4. branch

### 5. leaf

### 6. root

### 7. trunk

### 8. shade

### 9. to grow

| 1. 树 | 2. 灌木 | 3. 植物 |
| --- | --- | --- |
| 4. 枝 | 5. 叶 | 6. 根 |
| 7. 树干 | 8. 树荫 | 9. 成长 |

大自然 · 植物

# Nature · Plants

**1. cactus**

**2. palm tree**

**3. pine tree**

**4. flower**

**5. thorn**

**6. stem**

**7. seed**

**8. soil**

**9. pot**

| | | |
|---|---|---|
| 1. 仙人掌 | 2. 棕榈树 | 3. 松树 |
| 4. 花 | 5. 刺 | 6. 茎 |
| 7. 种子 | 8. 土壤 | 9. 壶/罐 |

大自然 · 植物

# Nature · Earth

**1. Earth**

**2. land**
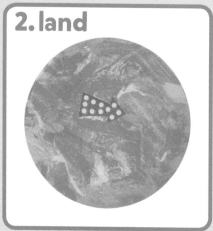

**3. mountain**

**4. desert**

**5. jungle**

**6. forest**

**7. island**

**8. hill**

**9. valley**

| 1. 地球 | 2. 土地 | 3. 山 |
| --- | --- | --- |
| 4. 沙漠 | 5. 丛林 | 6. 森林 |
| 7. 岛 | 8. 小山 | 9. 山谷 |

大自然 · 地球

# Nature · Earth

**1. ocean**

**2. river**

**3. lake**

**4. waterfall**

**5. beach**

**6. wave**

**7. mud**

**8. sand**

**9. rock**

| 1. 海洋 | 2. 河 | 3. 湖 |
| 4. 瀑布 | 5. 海滩 | 6. 波浪 |
| 7. 泥 | 8. 沙子 | 9. 岩 |

大自然 · 地球

# Nature · Space

**1. planet**

**2. stars**

**3. comet**

**4. sun**

**5. moon**

**6. satellite**

**7. astronaut**

**8. alien**

**9. to explore**

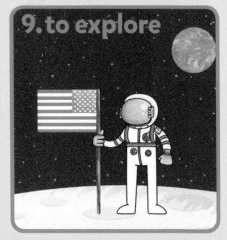

| | | |
|---|---|---|
| 1. 行星 | 2. 星 | 3. 彗星 |
| 4. 太阳 | 5. 月亮 | 6. 卫星 |
| 7. 宇航员 | 8. 外星人 | 9. 探索 |

大自然 · 太空

# Nature • Weather

**1. day**

**2. night**

**3. morning**

**4. spring**

**5. summer**

**6. afternoon**

**7. fall**

**8. winter**

**9. evening**

| | | |
|---|---|---|
| 1. 白天 | 2. 夜晚 | 3. 上午 |
| 4. 春季 | 5. 夏季 | 6. 下午 |
| 7. 秋季 | 8. 冬季 | 9. 晚上 |

大自然 • 天气

# Nature · Weather

### 1. rain

### 2. lightning

### 3. storm

### 4. sky

### 5. cloud

### 6. snow

### 7. fog

### 8. puddle

### 9. umbrella

| 1. 雨 | 2. 闪电 | 3. 风暴 |
| --- | --- | --- |
| 4. 天空 | 5. 云 | 6. 雪 |
| 7. 雾 | 8. 水坑 | 9. 雨伞 |

大自然 · 天气

# Nature · Weather

**1. hot**

**2. warm**

**3. cold**

**4. temperature**

**5. to melt**

**6. to freeze**

**7. sunny**

**8. cloudy**

**9. windy**

| 1. 热的 | 2. 暖的 | 3. 冷的 |
| 4. 温度 | 5. 融化 | 6. 冻结 |
| 7. 晴朗的 | 8. 多云的 | 9. 有风的 |

大自然 · 天气

# Nature · Environment

**1. tornado**

**2. volcano**

**3. tidal wave**

**4. hurricane**

**5. flood**

**6. avalanche**

**7. wildfire**

**8. drought**

**9. earthquake**

1. 龙卷风　　2. 火山　　3. 潮汐波

4. 飓风　　5. 洪水　　6. 雪崩

7. 野火　　8. 干旱　　9. 地震

大自然 · 环境

# Nature • Environment

**1. to help**

**2. to rescue**

**3. to take**

**4. to give**

**5. to share**

1. 帮助

2. 救援

3. 获取

4. 给与

5. 分享

大自然 • 环境

# Nature · Environment

## 1. to recycle

## 2. to litter

## 3. to use
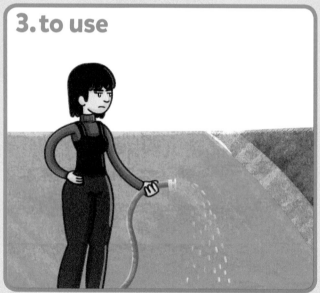

## 4. to waste

## 5. pollution

1. 回收

2. 扔垃圾

3. 使用

4. 浪费

5. 污染

大自然 · 环境

# Chapter 10
# Animals

第十章
动物

# Animals · Farm

**1. cow**

**2. pig**

**3. chicken**

**4. donkey**

**5. horse**

**6. turkey**

**7. goat**

**8. sheep**

**9. farm**

| 1. 奶牛 | 2. 猪 | 3. 鸡 |
|---|---|---|
| 4. 驴 | 5. 马 | 6. 火鸡 |
| 7. 山羊 | 8. 绵羊 | 9. 农场 |

动物 · 农场

# Animals · Ocean

**1. fish**

**2. shark**

**3. squid**

**4. octopus**

**5. crab**

**6. whale**

**7. dolphin**

**8. seal**

**9. to swim**

| 1. 鱼 | 2. 鲨鱼 | 3. 乌贼 |
| --- | --- | --- |
| 4. 章鱼 | 5. 螃蟹 | 6. 鲸 |
| 7. 海豚 | 8. 海豹 | 9. 游泳 |

动物 · 海洋

# Animals · Forest

### 1. bear

### 2. raccoon

### 3. porcupine

### 4. deer

### 5. skunk

### 6. wolf

### 7. fur

### 8. cave

### 9. to howl

| | | |
|---|---|---|
| 1. 熊 | 2. 臭鼬 | 3. 豪猪 |
| 4. 鹿 | 5. 臭鼬 | 6. 狼 |
| 7. 毛皮 | 8. 洞穴 | 9. 嚎叫 |

动物 · 森林

# Animals · Jungle

**1. panda**

**2. lion**

**3. crocodile**

**4. monkey**

**5. elephant**

**6. snake**

**7. giraffe**

**8. zebra**

**9. camel**

1. 熊猫

2. 狮子

3. 鳄鱼

4. 猴

5. 象

6. 蛇

7. 长颈鹿

8. 斑马

9. 骆驼

动物 · 丛林

# Animals · Birds

## 1. bird

## 2. wing

## 3. beak

## 4. feather

## 5. claw
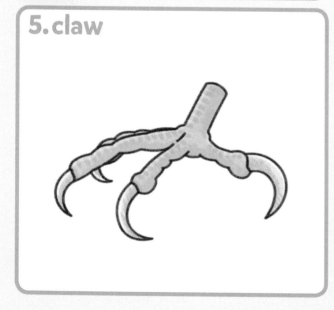

1. 鸟

2. 翅膀

3. 喙

4. 羽毛

5. 爪

# Animals · Birds

**1. eagle**

**2. owl**

**3. duck**

**4. penguin**

**5. peacock**

**6. hummingbird**

**7. flamingo**

**8. nest**

**9. to fly**

| 1. 鹰 | 2. 猫头鹰 | 3. 鸭 |
| --- | --- | --- |
| 4. 企鹅 | 5. 孔雀 | 6. 蜂鸟 |
| 7. 火烈鸟 | 8. 巢 | 9. 飞 |

动物 · 鸟

# Animals · Pets

**1. dog**

**2. puppy**

**3. lizard**

**4. cat**

**5. kitten**

**6. frog**

**7. rabbit**

**8. goldfish**

**9. turtle**

| | | |
|---|---|---|
| 1. 狗 | 2. 小狗 | 3. 蜥蜴 |
| 4. 猫 | 5. 小猫 | 6. 青蛙 |
| 7. 兔子 | 8. 金鱼 | 9. 海龟 |

动物 · 宠物

# Animals · Pets

### 1. leash

### 2. collar

### 3. aquarium

### 4. cage
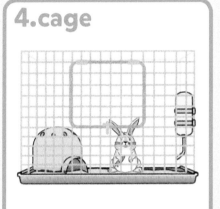

### 5. to feed

### 6. to pet

### 7. to chase

### 8. to train

### 9. to walk

| 1. 皮带 | 2. 项圈 | 3. 水族馆 |
| --- | --- | --- |
| 4. 笼子 | 5. 喂养 | 6. 抚摸 |
| 7. 追逐 | 8. 训练 | 9. 走 |

动物 · 宠物

# Animals · Insects

**1. bee**

**2. mosquito**

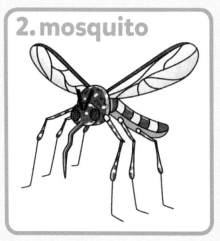

**3. fly**

**4. butterfly**

**5. spider**

**6. web**

**7. ant**

**8. snail**

**9. shell**

| 1. 蜜蜂 | 2. 蚊子 | 3. 苍蝇 |
|---|---|---|
| 4. 蝴蝶 | 5. 蜘蛛 | 6. 蜘蛛网 |
| 7. 蚂蚁 | 8. 蜗牛 | 9. 贝壳 |

# Glossary

# Glossary

## C

# Glossary

D

# Glossary

词汇表

# Glossary

# Glossary

# Glossary

# Glossary

## O

## P

# Glossary

# Glossary

# Glossary

## T

# Glossary

# Glossary

X

词汇表